GUITAR SONG TRAX 3

	Page#	CD Track

(Call It) Stormy Monday . . . . 5 . . . . 1-2 (minus guitar)

Europa . . . . 14 . . . . 3-4 (minus guitar)

Look at Little Sister . . . . 20 . . . . 5-6 (minus guitar)

Proud Mary . . . . 31 . . . . 7-8 (minus guitar)

Refugee . . . . 36 . . . . 9-10 (minus guitar)

Born Under a Bad Sign . . . . 42 . . . . 11-12 (minus guitar)

Editor: Aaron Stang
Cover Design: Frank Milone & Ken Rehm
Photography: Roberto Santos
Sound Recording: Daniel Warner & Lee Levin

Performance Notes

(Call It) Stormy Monday
(But Tuesday's Just As Bad)

Words and Music by
Aron T. Walker

"Stormy Monday" is one of the most popular blues standards ever written. Virtually every blues guitarist plays this song. The original version is by T. Bone Walker. The Allman Brothers also have an extremely well known version.

The basic rhythm riff is based around a three note 9th chord. The 9th chord is a common substitution for a dominant 7th chord. The real sound of this riff is based on starting each 9th chord a whole step (2 frets) above and sliding down. If we were to analyze this movement, the first chord is technically a 13th chord resolving down to a 9th chord. So, if we were to name each chord, the progression would be G13 to G9, C13 to C9, etc.

Like "Look at Little Sister," this song is written in 12/8: 12 beats per measure and an 8th note gets one beat. Don't let that confuse you; this is just like any rock shuffle: There are 4 strong beats, each divided in 3 parts. So, a measure of 12/8 is just like a measure of 4/4 where each beat is a triplet. For example:

In 4/4: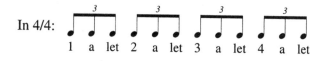

In 12/8: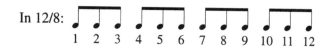

Both rhythms would sound exactly the same.

This is an "uptown" blues, meaning the chord progression is a little more sophisticated than some. For example, "Born Under a Bad Sign" calls for a straightforward blues sound—mostly minor pentatonic; but "Stormy Monday" allows for a much more flexible approach to the solo. You can use just G minor pentatonic to start, but you should also try to experiment with blues scales that mix major and minor pentatonic together.

See pages 46 - 57 of *Guitar Rock Shop 3* for more information on blues scales and soloing over an "uptown" blues.
See pages 10 and 22 of *Guitar Method 3* or pages 8 and 12 of *Guitar Rock Shop 3* for more information on barre chords.

Europa

Music by
Carlos Santana and Tom Coster

This classic guitar instrumental was written and originally recorded by Carlos Santana. It was also a huge hit for jazz saxophonist Gato Barbieri.

To get that beautiful Carlos Santana tone, I suggest using a guitar with humbucking pick-ups. Experiment with playing the lead on your "rhythm" or "neck" pick-up, although Carlos manages to achieve his singing, signature warm sound on both the rhythm and lead (bridge) pick-ups. If you have a wah-wah pedal you can also try using it as a tone control—just position the pedal so that it filters out some of the highs and leave it in that position; don't rock it back and forth while you are playing.

The rhythm guitar part to this song uses a variety of open and barre chord formations, all played with a simple arpeggio pattern. Try using a chorus pedal on this part.

This song is in C minor. Use C minor and C minor pentatonic scales to improvise the solo at measure 36. C minor is the relative minor to E♭ major so transpose the major scale fingerings you've learned to E♭.

Guitar 1 (lead guitar): *Guitar Method 3*, see the "Exploring the Neck" sections and Rock Workshops 301 and 302 for the scale fingerings required to improvise a solo. Also see *Rock Shop 3* pages 36 - 37.

Guitar 2 (rhythm guitar): See pages 10 -11 and 22 - 23 of *Guitar Method 3* or pages 8 - 9 and 12 - 13 of *Rock Shop 3*.

Look at Little Sister

Words and Music by
Hank Ballard

"Look at Little Sister" is a classic rock and roll boogie pattern in E. This version is based on Stevie Ray Vaughan's immortal recording of the song. The basic riff, with the addition of a few twists to add some spice, is the same boogie pattern we've played throughout the *Guitar Method* and *Guitar Rock Shop* series.

The song is written in 12/8: 12 beats per measure and an 8th note gets one beat. Don't let that confuse you; this is just like any rock shuffle: there are 4 strong beats, each divided in 3 parts. So, a measure of 12/8 is just like a measure of 4/4 where each beat is a triplet. For example:

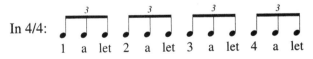

Both rhythms would sound exactly the same.

For information and licks you can use in the solo section, see the blues/rock soloing section of *Guitar Rock Shop 3* (beginning on page 46) and all of the Rock Workshops in *Guitar Method 2 and 3*.

Proud Mary

Words and Music by
J.C. Fogerty

"Proud Mary" is in the key of D. The classic chord progression to this song can be played with either "open" position chord fingerings (as shown in the arrangement) or entirely with barre chords. After learning the rhythm part as written, try playing it with only barre chords.

See page 30 of *Guitar Method 3* for more information on playing in the key of D.
See pages 10 and 22 of *Guitar Method 3* or pages 8 and 12 of *Guitar Rock Shop 3* for more information on barre chords.

Refugee

Words and Music by
Tom Petty and Michael Campbell

"Refugee" is a classic rock tune in F# minor. Remember, F# minor is the relative minor to A major. In F# minor we use the same key signature as A major (F#, C# and G#), which means we use basically the same chords and scales as in A—only centering around F#.

See page 34 of *Guitar Method 3* for more information on playing in the key of F# minor and page 36 of *Guitar Rock Shop 3* for more information on soloing in minor keys.

Born Under a Bad Sign

Words and Music by
William Bell and Booker T. Jones

"Born Under a Bad Sign" has become a blues standard. The original classic version is by Albert King. Plus, the song has been covered by Eric Clapton and Jimi Hendrix.

"Born Under a Bad Sign" is a blues in G. The core of the song is a simple, unison, minor pentatonic bass and guitar riff (see Intro and Chorus) with a variation on the riff in the Verse. I suggest using G minor pentatonic for the soloing section. One interesting feature of the basic riff is the chromatic chord section. These are just simple three-note dominant seventh chords sliding up and down one fret at a time (see bar 9 and bars 34 - 37).

See page 30 of *Guitar Rock Shop 3* for more information on minor pentatonic soloing.

(Call It) Stormy Monday
(But Tuesday's Just As Bad)

Words and Music by
ARON T. WALKER

(Call It) Stormy Monday - 9 - 1

1. They call it storm-y Mon-day, but

2.3. *See additional lyrics*

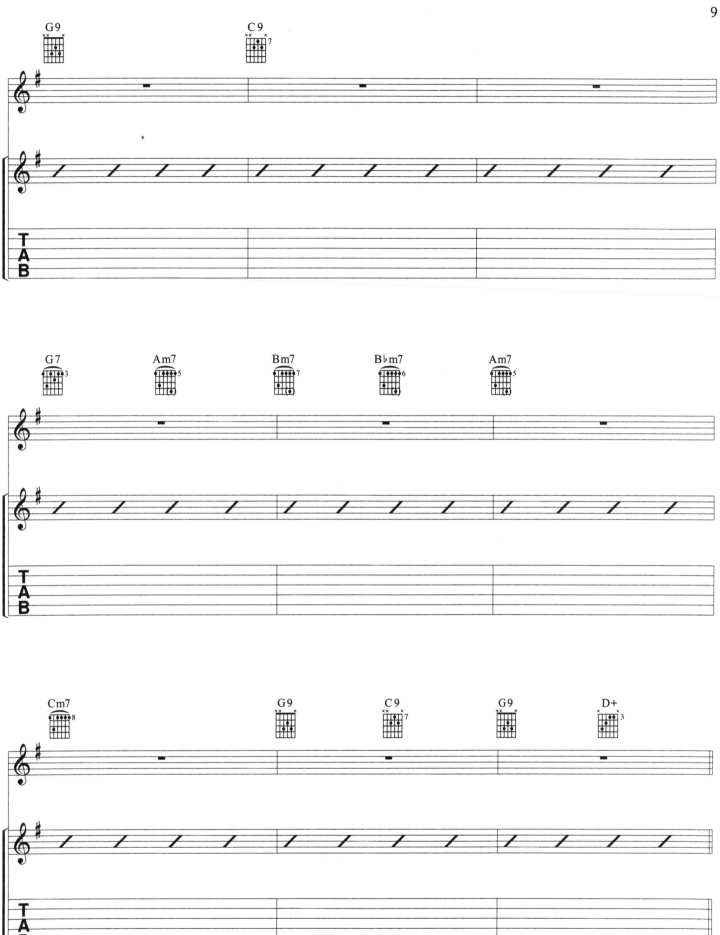

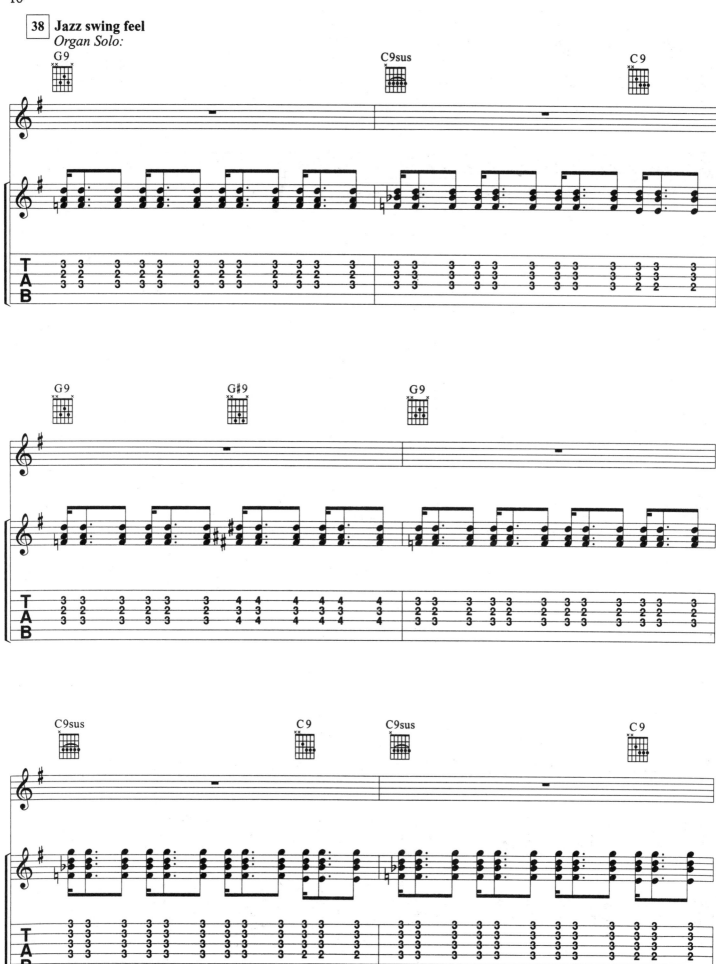

12

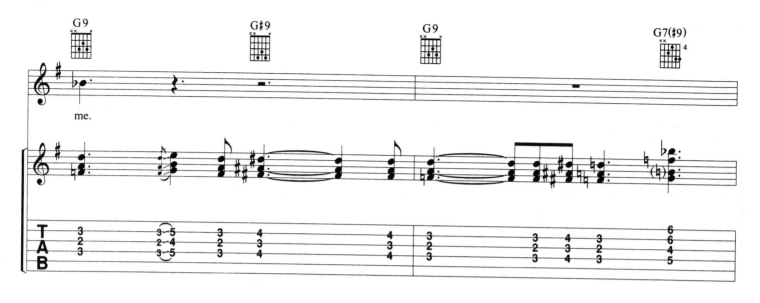

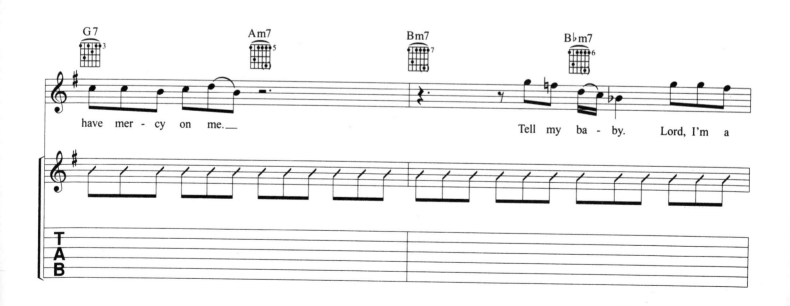

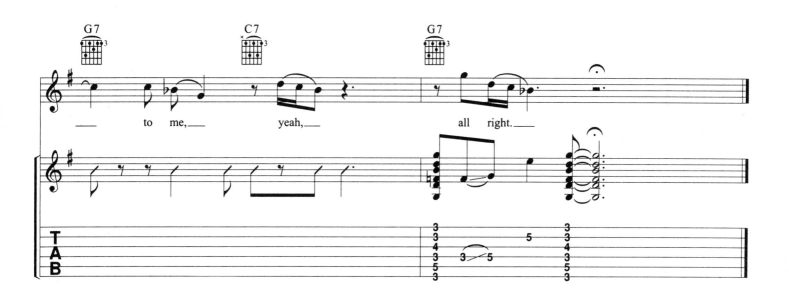

Verse 2:
The eagle flies on Friday,
Saturday I go out to play.
The eagle flies on Friday,
Saturday I go out to play.
Sunday I go to church,
Lord, and I kneel down and pray.

Verse 3:
Lord, have mercy,
Lord, have mercy on me.
Lord, have mercy,
Lord, have mercy on me.
And though I'm tryin', tryin' to find my baby,
Won't somebody please send her home?

Europa
(Earth's Cry Heaven's Smile)

Music by
CARLOS SANTANA
and TOM COSTER

Moderately slow ♩ = 76

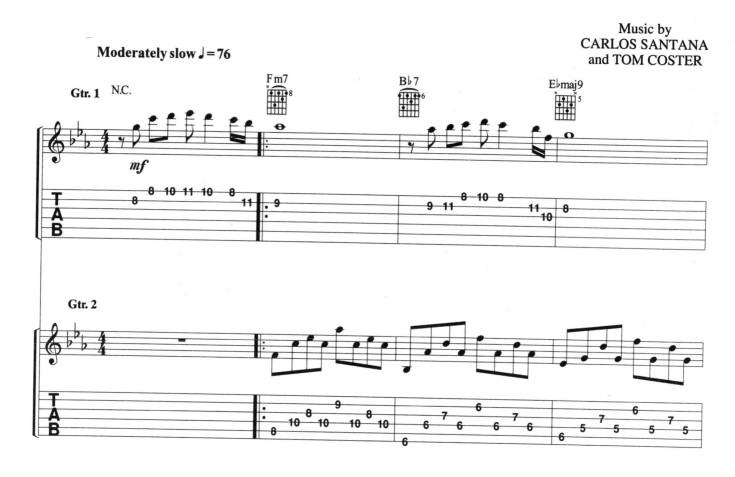

Europa - 6 - 1

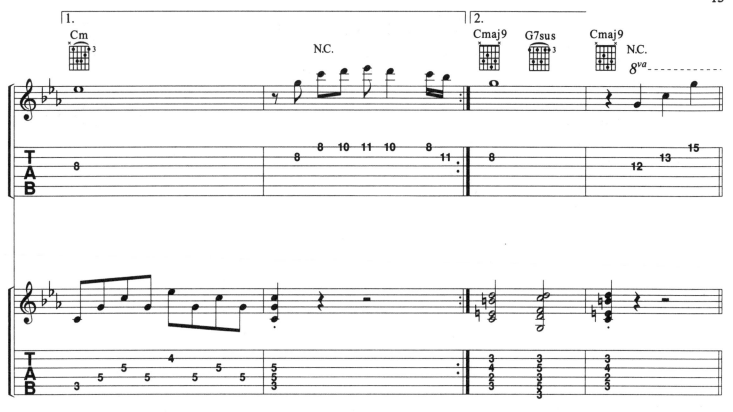

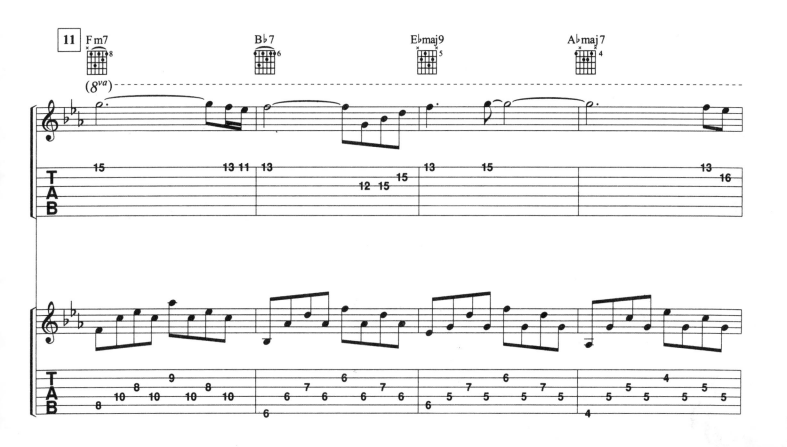

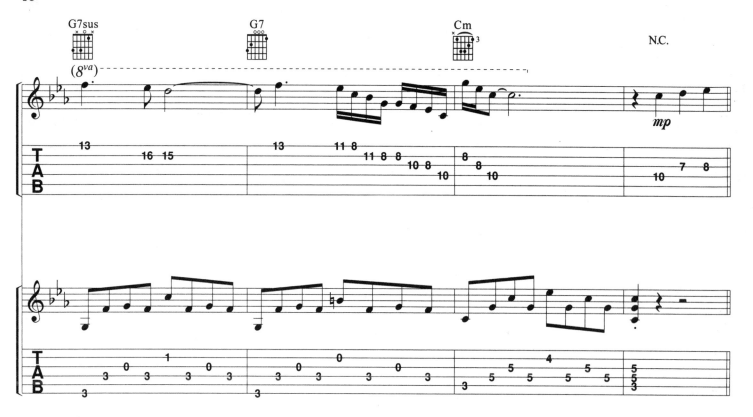

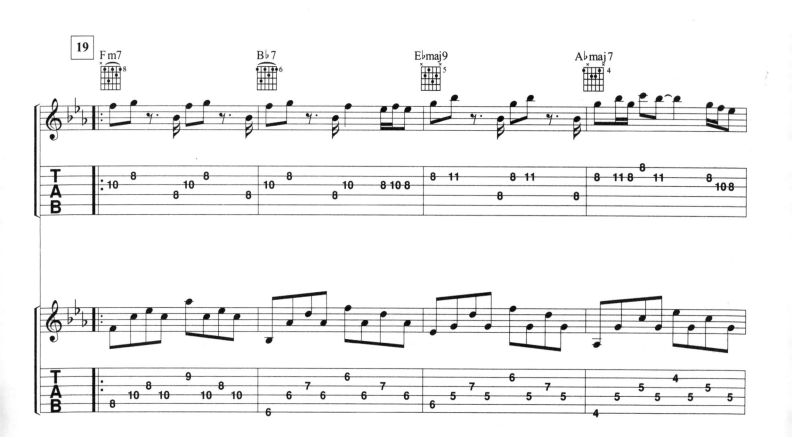

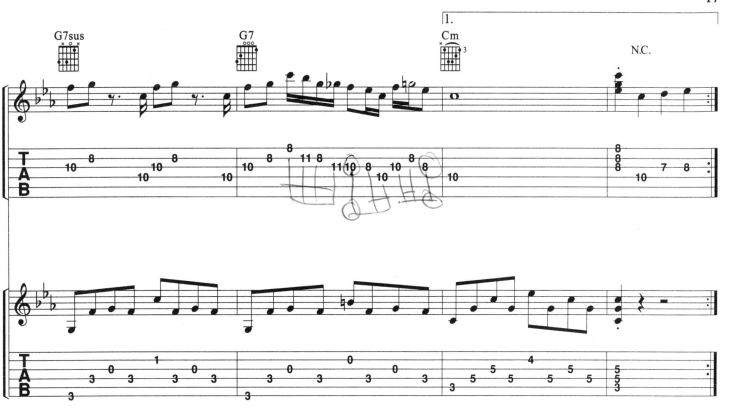

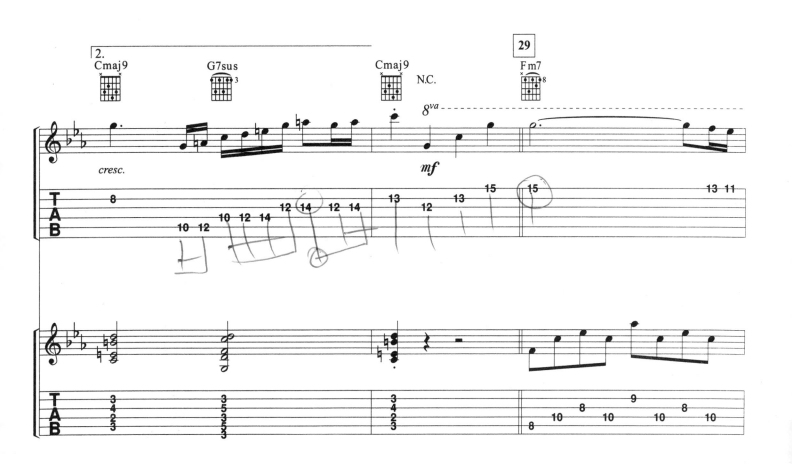

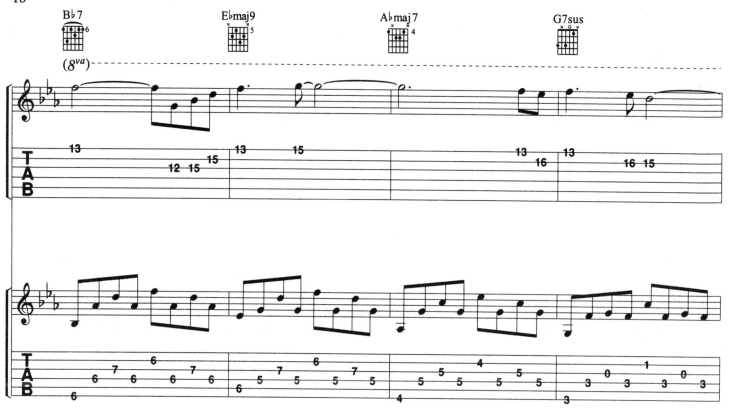

35 *Solo Section:*

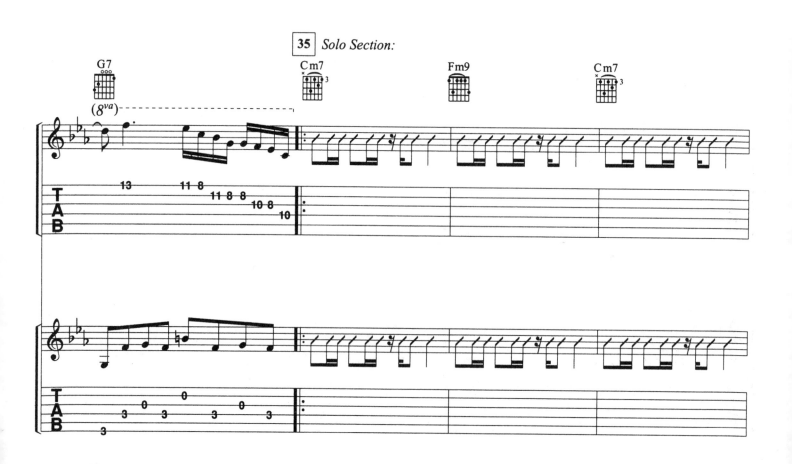

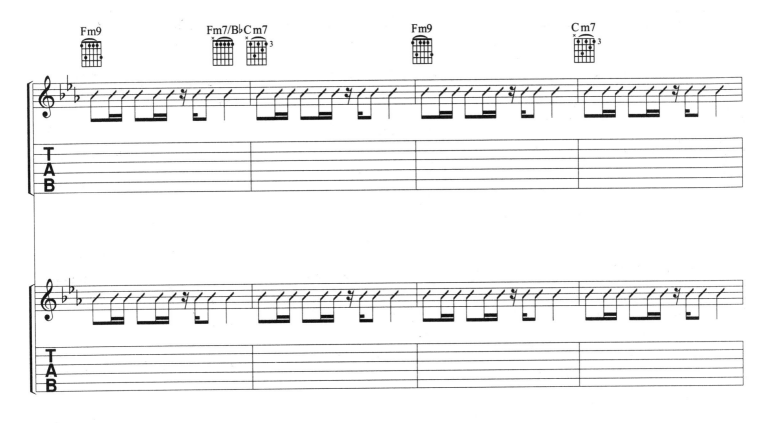

Look At Little Sister

Words and Music by
HANK BALLARD

Look at Little Sister - 11 - 1

2. What a - bout the neigh - bors? What they gon - na say?

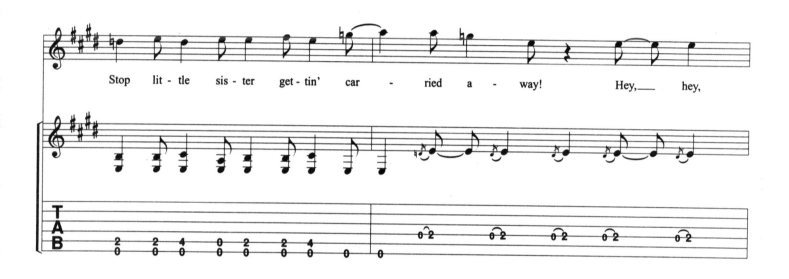

Stop lit - tle sis - ter get - tin' car - ried a - way! Hey,___ hey,

hey, look at lit - tle sis -

23

Look at Little Sister - 11 - 4

24

Look at Little Sister - 11 - 5

37 *Solo Section:*

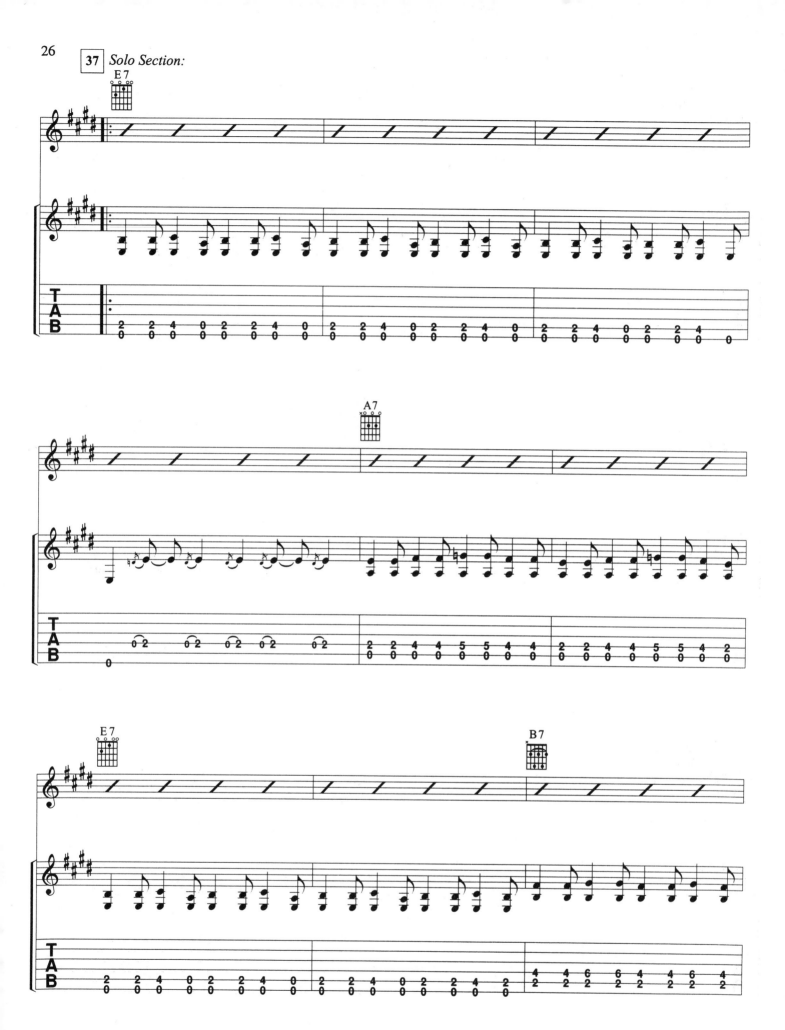

Look at Little Sister - 11 - 9

Proud Mary

Words and Music by
J.C. FOGERTY

Moderate rock ♩ = 126

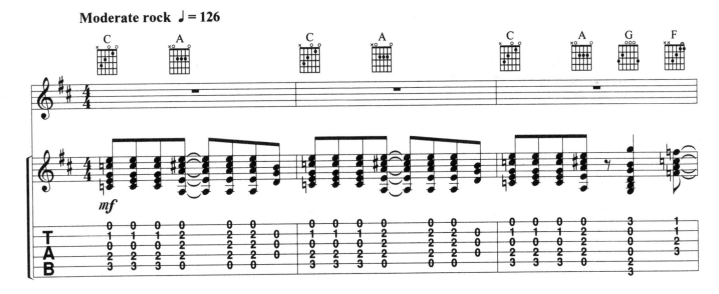

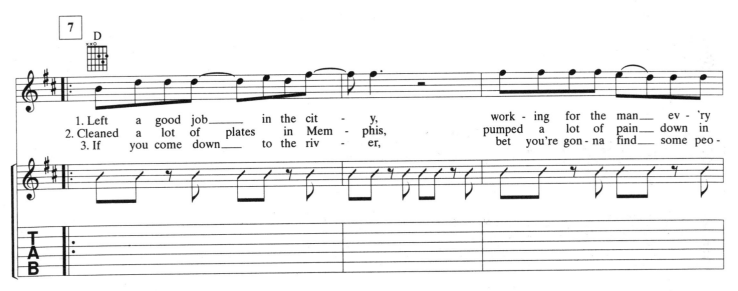

1. Left a good job in the cit - y, working for the man ev - 'ry
2. Cleaned a lot of plates in Mem - phis, pumped a lot of pain down in
3. If you come down to the riv - er, bet you're gon - na find some peo -

Proud Mary - 5 - 1

32

Proud Mary - 5 - 2

34

Coda

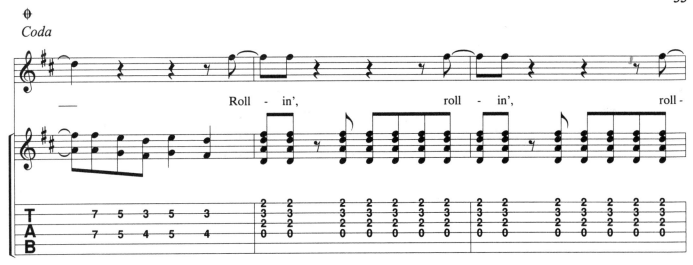

Roll - in',   roll - in',   roll -

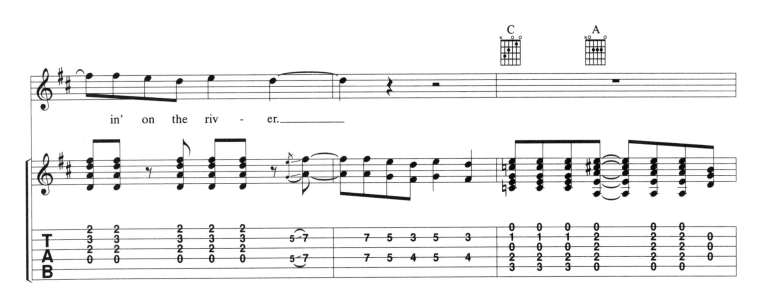

in' on the riv - er.

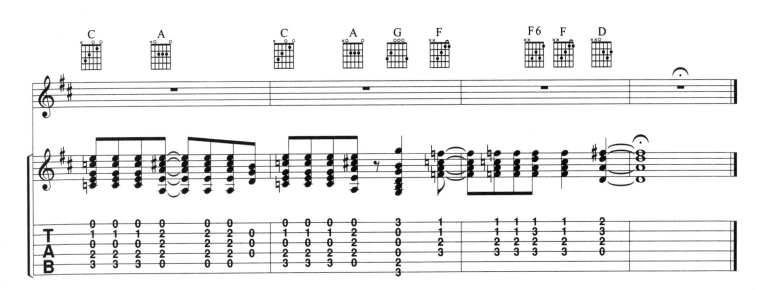

Proud Mary - 5 - 5

Refugee

Words and Music by
TOM PETTY and
MICHAEL CAMPBELL

Refugee - 6 - 1

9 𝄋 *Verse:*

1. We got some-thin', we both know it, we don't talk too much a-bout___ it.
2.3. *See additional lyrics*

Ain't no real___ big se - cret, all the same, some - how we get a -

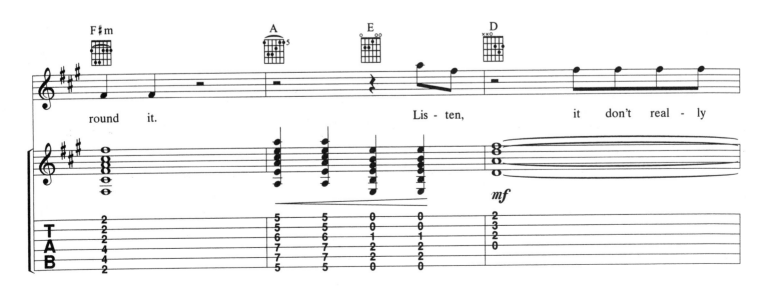

round it. Lis - ten, it don't real - ly

mat - ter to me,___ ba - by. You be - lieve what you want to be - lieve.___ You see you

21 *Chorus:*

don't___ have___ to live like a ref - u - gee. Don't have to live like a

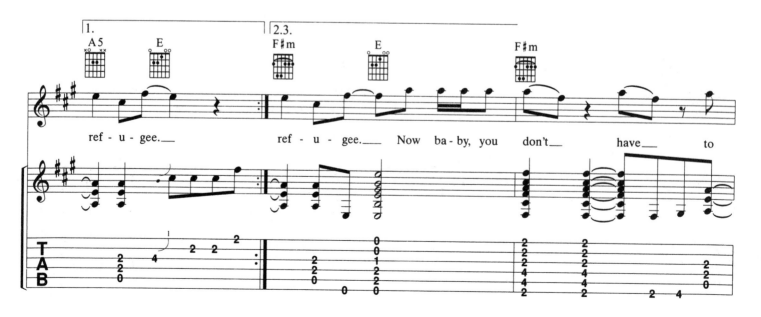

ref - u - gee.___ ref - u - gee.___ Now ba - by, you don't___ have___ to

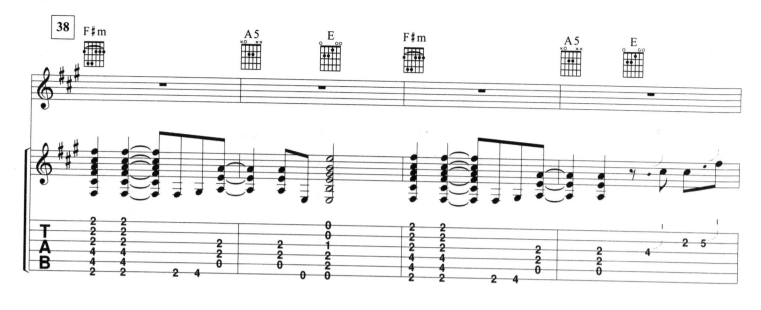

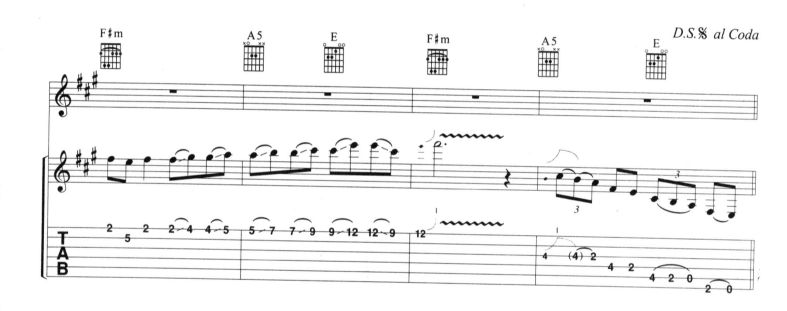

D.S. % al Coda

ref - u - gee.__ You don't__ have__ to live like a ref - u - gee.

41

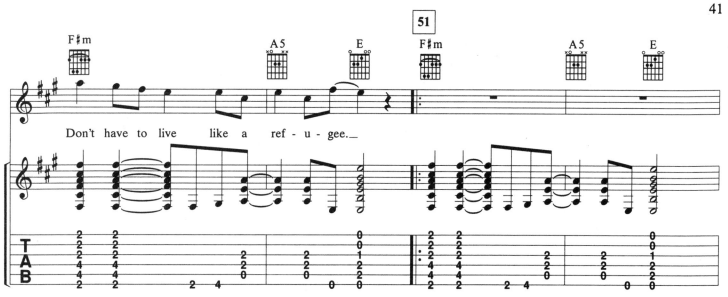

Don't have to live like a ref - u - gee.__

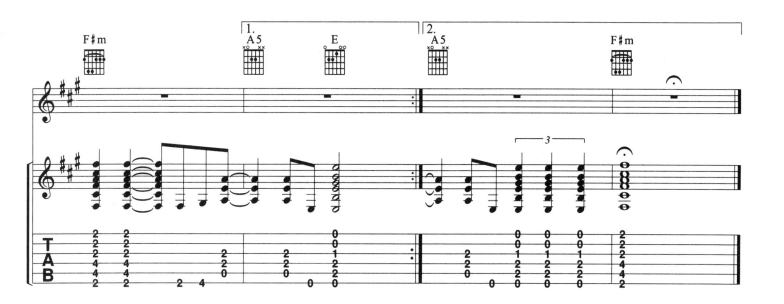

Verse 2:
Somewhere, somehow, somebody must have
Kicked you around some.
Tell me why you wanna lay there,
Revel in your abandon.
It don't make no difference to me, baby.
Everybody's had to fight to be free.
(To Chorus:)

Verse 3:
Somewhere, somehow, somebody must have
Kicked you around some.
Who knows, maybe you were kidnapped, tied up,
Taken away and held for ransom.
It don't really matter to me, baby.
Everybody's had to fight to be free.
(To Chorus:)

Refugee - 6 - 6

Born Under A Bad Sign

Words and Music by
WILLIAM BELL and
BOOKER T. JONES

Moderate ♩ = 92

5 *Chorus:*

Born un-der a bad sign,

I've been down since I be-gan to crawl. If it was-n't for bad___ luck,

Born Under a Bad Sign - 6 - 1

13 *Verses 1 & 2:*

1. Bad luck and trou-ble's my on-ly friend,_ I've been down_ ev-er since
2. *See additional lyrics*

I was ten.___ Born un-der a bad sign,

simile

44

26 *Guitar Solo:*

46

Born Under a Bad Sign - 6 - 5

all.___

Born un-der a bad sign.

Born un-der a bad sign.

rit.

Verse 2:
Oh, wine and women
Is all I crave.
Big, bad woman a-gonna carry me to my grave.
Born under a bad sign,
I've been down since I began to crawl.
If it wasn't for bad luck,
I wouldn't have no luck at all.

GUITAR TAB GLOSSARY **

TABLATURE EXPLANATION

READING TABLATURE: Tablature illustrates the six strings of the guitar. Notes and chords are indicated by the placement of fret numbers on a given string(s).

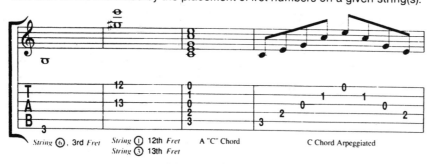

String ⑥, 3rd Fret   String ① 12th Fret   A "C" Chord   C Chord Arpeggiated
String ③ 13th Fret

BENDING NOTES

HALF STEP: Play the note and bend string one half step.*

PREBEND AND RELEASE: Bend the string, play it, then release to the original note.

WHOLE STEP: Play the note and bend string one whole step.

RHYTHM SLASHES

STRUM INDICATIONS: Strum with indicated rhythm. The chord voicings are found on the first page of the transcription underneath the song title.

INDICATING SINGLE NOTES USING RHYTHM SLASHES: Very often single notes are incorporated into a rhythm part. The note name is indicated above the rhythm slash with a fret number and a string indication.

*A half step is the smallest interval in Western music; it is equal to one fret. A whole step equals two frets.

**By Kenn Chipkin and Aaron Stang

ARTICULATIONS

HAMMER ON: Play lower note, then "hammer on" to higher note with another finger. Only the first note is attacked.

PULL OFF: Play higher note, then "pull off" to lower note with another finger. Only the first note is attacked.

LEGATO SLIDE: Play note and slide to the following note. (Only first note is attacked).

PALM MUTE: The note or notes are muted by the palm of the pick hand by lightly touching the string(s) near the bridge.

ACCENT: Notes or chords are to be played with added emphasis.

DOWN STROKES AND UPSTROKES: Notes or chords are to be played with either a downstroke (⊓) or upstroke (∨) of the pick.